Before the throne of grace

Before the Throne of Grace

∞

Pressing into His Presence

31 Days of Daily Reflections

By Chinwe L. Ezueh Okpalaoka

Before the Throne of Grace: Pressing into His Presence
31 Days of Daily Reflections

© Copyright 2017

Cover art "Resurrecting" by Chineze Okpalaoka

Front and back cover design by Miosotys Nunez & Chineze Okpalaoka

The Solid Rock by Edward Mote, ca. 1834: Copyright Public domain

Published by CLEO Books

ISBN-13:978-0692953655 (Chinwe Okpalaoka)

ISBN-10:0692953655

_____

*Let us therefore come boldly to the
throne of grace, that we may obtain mercy
and find grace to help in time of need*
(Hebrews 4:16, NKJV)

DEDICATION

I dedicate this book to my father, Dr. Micah Ikechukwu Ezueh, who passed on to glory on August 30, 2015. Daddy, I know you are resting in peace. You have not been forgotten.

ACKNOWLEDGMENTS

I am very thankful for the family and friends I am blessed to have in my life. You have been supportive of my bringing these words to paper. I want to begin by thanking my covenant partner and husband, Osita Okpalaoka, and our children, Ugonna, Chineze, Dubem and Amara, for your sure love and encouragement. Thank you for believing in me always. I thank my Mother, Cecilia Ezueh, my sisters, Nkem and Ngozi, and brother, Ik who patiently allow me to preach to them at every opportunity I get. As Nkem recently reminded me, we are bound by God's covenant. Thank you, Chineze, for your second book cover work for me. Your cover art captures how I long to approach God's throne of grace every time. I am grateful to Pat Ikegwuonu who was the first to know when this book was just a thought and would periodically check in on its progress. Sephora Escarpeta-Garcia, Twana Young, Miosotys Nunez and Christy Bolaji, thanks for your reviews and for encouraging me when I did not want to let the book out of my hands. Christy, I am sure you can hear our many conversations through these pages. Miosotys, thanks for the design of the front and back covers. David Roy, you have been a spiritual friend and mentor and have witnessed my growth pains. Thanks for your prayers. Finally, to Angelett Anderson, it was God who brought us together and I thank Him for you.

AUTHOR'S NOTE

∞

Before the Throne of Grace: Pressing into His Presence has been years in the making. The title describes the posture with which we approach God and His Word in our private study times. I have been writing off and on throughout the years and kept putting off my dreams of completing one or more devotionals. I use several devotionals during my Bible study time and have found them to be very insightful, enriching and rewarding. Devotionals encourage the discipline of regular Bible reading and reflection and I hope that this one offers the same experience to the reader. I have included opportunities for reflection at the end of each day. I hope you pause for a moment to meditate on what you have read. The Holy Spirit is your teacher and He will reveal the enduring truth of God's Word as you earnestly seek Him.

To honor God, Jesus Christ, and the Holy Spirit, I have capitalized the first letter in the pronouns, He, Him, His, and Himself except where they are used otherwise in direct quotes.

DAY ONE

The Macedonian call: when God diverts you from a good cause

"The Holy Spirit had prevented them from preaching the Word in the province of Asia."
(Acts 16:6, NLT)

∞

Studying Paul's second missionary journey with Silas, I noticed that the Holy Spirit forbade them to preach the Word in Asia and Bithynia (Acts 16:6) – (good cause, wrong timing). Instead, the Holy Spirit directed them to Macedonia after Paul saw a vision of a Macedonian man calling to them for help. We are not told that they questioned God about His reasons for redirecting their journey. Instead, we learn that they obeyed and departed immediately for Macedonia (Acts 16:10). We have heard it said that where God calls us He keeps us, but we are not promised that there will be no trials and tribulations in our obedience to the call. In fact, Jesus assures us that, in this world, we will experience trials and tribulations, but that we should take heart because He has deprived the world of the power to harm us (John 16:33).

That is what Paul and Silas would soon learn in Philippi, a capital city of Macedonia. It would have been easy for Paul and Silas to expect a worry-free missionary journey. After all, they were in the will of God; instead, they would encounter much trial. How many times have we expected a smooth ride because we are walking in the will of God?

As I continued reading, I realized that there was a purpose for the diversion to Macedonia. It was much more than to fellowship with Lydia and the other women who worshipped God and met regularly for prayer. It was also much more than to deliver the damsel who was possessed of the spirit of divination. For doing the Lord's work in Macedonia, Paul and Silas were brought to the very place God had ordained for them to be – in the jailhouse. And they did not lose sight of the assurance they previously had in Acts 16:10 – that they were in Macedonia by and in the will of God. Perhaps that is why they could sing while in jail at the midnight hour. They knew that the Lord who had diverted them to Macedonia must have a purpose in spite of their trials.

In fact, these trials were not new to Paul and Silas. Paul had stated that *"...we must through much tribulation enter into the kingdom of God"* (Acts 14:22, KJV). Therefore, they were not shaken by their circumstance. Instead of questioning God, Paul and Silas praised Him in the sight of the jailor and other prisoners. As they praised Him for their assured deliverance, God's purpose for their situation became clear. You see, there was a certain jailor who had to witness, firsthand, the delivering power of God. He had to see the manner in which God's power would disrupt the normal routine in the jail.

If Paul and Silas had disobeyed God and gone on to Asia and Bithynia, they would have been doing God's work alright, but they would have been walking in disobedience. They would have missed a God-opportunity to save a young girl, a jailor and his household. The purpose of the divine earthquake that shook up the jail was not to release Paul, Silas and the other prisoners from jail because, as Scripture tells us, they were all still there when the earthquake was over. They did not escape at the first opportunity they had. There was a greater purpose which became apparent when the jailor asked, *"Sirs, what must I do to be saved?"* (Acts 16:30, KJV). And Paul responded, *"Believe in the Lord Jesus*

Christ and you shall be saved, you and your household" (Acts 16:31, KJV). With that simple question, salvation came to the jailor and his household.

We can learn from this story that God can sometimes divert us from a good cause and that the fact that we are walking in obedience to God's will does not eliminate trials from our path. Instead, if we have the assurance that we are led by the Holy Spirit of the living God, then we will look beyond the trials that come to distract us and keep our eyes on the higher purpose of God in every situation, being mindful that *"all things work together for good to those who love God, to those who are the called according to His purpose"* (Romans 8: 28, KJV).

Pause for reflection: Have you ever found yourself having to choose between doing a good thing and a God thing? What did you choose to do and why?

DAY TWO

Unity in prayer is power

*"Behold, how good and how pleasant it is for
brethren to dwell together in unity."*
(Psalm 133:1, KJV)

∞

Brethren, there is physical and spiritual strength in unity.
Amos 3:3 (KJV) asks, *"Can two walk together except they be
agreed?"* Also Ecclesiastes 4:12 (KJV) reminds us that two
are better than one for each will support the other– *"though
a man might prevail against him who is alone, two will
withstand him."* All this is as true spiritually as it is physically.
Even the Psalmist declares:

> *Behold, how good and how pleasant it is for
> brethren to dwell together in unity! It is like the
> precious ointment upon the head, that ran down
> upon the beard, even Aaron's beard: that went
> down to the skirts of his garments; As the dew of
> Hermon, and as the dew that descended upon the
> mountains of Zion: for there the Lord commanded
> the blessing, even life for evermore* (Psalm 133:1-
> 3, KJV).

Why does David liken unity among brethren to the precious
anointing oil that ran down Aaron's beard to the hem of his
priestly garment? A quick visit to the Old Testament helps
reveal the connection. When God wanted a tabernacle built
for Him so that His presence could dwell among His people,
he separated Moses from the children of Israel and hid him
in Mt. Sinai for 40 days and nights. It was here that He

gave Moses a pattern for the building of the tabernacle which was to come.

One of God's instructions to Moses was to set apart (consecrate) Aaron and his sons as priests unto God and anoint them with oil. The anointing oil was poured on their heads and, as we learn, it flowed all the way down to the hem of their priestly garments, saturating the whole body (Exodus 29:7; 30:30). The oil was symbolic of God's anointing power flowing from the head to the hem of the priest's garment. So, what the Psalmist is saying about unity and the anointing oil is that it is indeed pleasant (and pleasing in God's eyes) for those who are called by His name to dwell together in unity. Where there is unity, there is anointing power that saturates the body of Christ in much the same way that the anointing oil *"consecrated the whole body"* of Aaron and his sons from the crown of their heads to their feet (Psalm 133:2, AMPC).

Psalm 133:3 beautifully concludes with the reminder that it is in unity that our God COMMANDS the blessing forevermore (*emphasis is mine*). What is the blessing of God? God has promised to bless us in the work of our hands and with His presence in our midst; He has pronounced His blessing in our bodies, finances, and relationships. We have been assured that God's blessings will follow us if we seek diligently after Him and obey His commands (Deuteronomy 28). The Bible is replete with promises of God's blessings too numerous to recount here.

So, brethren, what are we waiting for? Jesus reminded His disciples that *"by this all will know that you are my disciples, if you have love for one another"* (John 13:35, NKJV). If we walk with one another in love, then we will walk together in one accord and with one purpose and we will pray and agree with one accord and one purpose. We will then be able to form a formidable force with which we can withstand the wicked wiles of the enemy (Ephesians 6:11). Where there is unity, there is anointing power! What is impossible for us to accomplish in the flesh is possible under the anointing–the anointing which breaks every yoke (Isaiah 10:27).

Pause for reflection: Can you remember a time when you experienced the power of God as a result of unity with other believers in prayer?

DAY THREE

Where does your trust lie?

"Some trust in chariots and some in horses,
but we trust in the name of the Lord our God."
(Psalm 20:7, NIV)

∞

The walls of Jerusalem had several watch towers from which watchmen diligently kept watch over the city. In those days, walls were built as fortresses to protect a city. From the watch towers, watchmen stayed awake and alert in shifts to discern from afar and announce the approaching enemy or friend. In addition to keeping the enemy out, the towers also served as places of refuge for city inhabitants (Judges 9:51). Today, intercessors have been called to serve as watchmen over our homes, churches, cities, nations and our world. Like the watchmen of old, we are called to take up our posts and be alert to the wicked wiles of the enemy who prowls like a lion waiting to see who he will devour (1 Peter 5:8). We are not and should not be ignorant of his wiles and intentions (2 Corinthians 2:11).

Brethren, we cannot sleep on the job because the enemy does not sleep on the job, but we have an advantage over him—the Lord God who is on our side. Psalm 127:1 reminds us that except the Lord keeps watch over the city, the watchman lies awake in vain. We are also assured that He who keeps Israel does not slumber nor sleep (Psalm 121:3-4). He is our ultimate high tower, our refuge and our strength. Only complete dependence on God will get us through the watch hour and one of the ways we can maintain our position is to call upon His name.

Proverbs 18:10 likens the name of our God to a strong tower into which we can run and be safe. His name is Jehovah; He is the great I AM. That means that He is anything we need Him to be in any situation. He is El-Shaddai, the all-sufficient God; He is Jehovah-Jireh, the God our provider; He is Jehovah Shammah, the God that is always there; and even Jehovah Sabaoth, the God of Hosts. Where do you find refuge in times of trouble? Where does your trust lie? Hopefully it is in the name of the Lord.

Sometimes we misplace our trust in the wrong things or the wrong people. The Psalmist declares that *"some trust in chariots and some in horses, but we trust in the name of the Lord our God"* (Psalm 20:7, NIV). We also learn that *"the rich think of their wealth as a strong defense; they imagine it to be a high wall of safety"* (Proverbs 18:11, NLT). This means that there are some who look to their wealth as their strong tower, as their fortified city, and as their refuge in times of trouble.

The righteous should know better than to boast in anything else but knowing God through His names. God Himself, speaking through Jeremiah cautions us:

> *Let not the wise boast of their wisdom or the strong boast of their strength or the rich boast of their riches, but let the one who boasts boast about this: that they have the understanding to know me, that I am the LORD, who exercises kindness, justice and righteousness on earth, for in these I delight, declares the Lord* (9:23-24, NIV).

Pause for reflection: So, brothers and sisters, in what or who do you place your trust? In whom do you boast?

DAY FOUR

The righteous are bold as lions

"Forgetting what lies behind and straining forward to what lies ahead, [we] press on toward the goal to win the [supreme and heavenly] prize to which God in Christ Jesus is calling us upward."
(Philippians 3:13-14, AMPC)

∞

Every New Year begins with the season of resolutions, of plans and strategies for new beginnings. The New Year brings promises of fresh starts and renewed hope. Depending on who you ask, statistics indicate that about 80 percent of people fail to keep their resolutions within the first two months of the year and gradually return to their old ways. It is no surprise, then, that this season is also one filled with condemnation and shame from feeling like we have failed *again*. Likewise, we can experience feelings of condemnation when we fall short of God's standards one more time and may beat ourselves up for failing over and over again. But the good news is that God's grace is more than enough for us (2 Corinthians 12:9). Paul offers this assurance:

> *Therefore, there is now no condemnation (no adjudging guilty of wrong) for those who are in Christ Jesus, who live [and] walk not after the dictates of the flesh, but after the dictates of the Spirit* (Romans 8:1, AMPC).

Rather than resign ourselves to never getting it right, we can look to God for help to begin again. He can help us forget the failures of the past and focus on beginning again.

He has invited us to ask with the assurance that we will receive from Him (Luke 11:9). But when we pray, we must not come before God with our heads bowed in shame for He wants us to:

> *Fearlessly and confidently and boldly draw near to the throne of grace (the throne of God's unmerited favor to us sinners), that we may receive mercy [for our failures] and find grace to help in good time for every need [appropriate help and well-timed help, coming just when we need it]* (Hebrews 4:16, AMPC).

If our earthly fathers know how to give good gifts to us, how much more our heavenly Father (Luke 11:13)? Therefore, if you are in need of a second chance, dare to approach God's throne with boldness, knowing that by His grace and mercy, you can do all things through Him who strengthens us (Philippians 4:13).

Pause for reflection: Have you ever felt that you have failed at keeping your promises to God or to others one too many times? Remember that, today, you can come boldly to Him without fear or condemnation and He will be your present help.

DAY FIVE

Unwavering faith: waiting on the promises of God

"For the vision is yet for an appointed time,
but at the end it shall speak, and not lie; though
it tarry, wait for it; because it will surely come, it
will not tarry."
(Habakkuk 2:3, KJV)

∞

Dear Saints,

Our God still speaks to His children today. Although He is the Ancient of Days, He still speaks through visions, dreams and prophecies as well as His Word. Speaking through the prophet Joel, God promised:

> *I will pour out my spirit upon all flesh; and your sons and your daughters shall prophesy, your old men shall dream dreams, your young men shall see visions: And also upon the servants and upon the handmaids in those days will I pour out my spirit* (Joel 2:28-29, KJV).

Our *"God is no respecter of persons"* (Acts 10:34, KJV). He will reveal Himself and His plans through the Holy Spirit to whosoever will hear Him. And because *"one day is with the Lord as a thousand years, and a thousand years as one day"* (2 Peter 3:8, KJV), and because His thoughts are not like our thoughts nor His ways like our ways (Isaiah 55:8), there is no timetable to the fulfillment of God's promises towards us.

> *God is not a man that He should lie; neither the son of man that He should repent: hath He said,*

and shall He not do it? Or hath He spoken, and shall He not make it good (Numbers 23:19, KJV)?

Like many saints, when I receive promises from God through visions, dreams or other people, I write them down and I wait, patiently (most of the time), for their fulfillment. At times, I get impatient and I revisit the promises to remind myself that God is faithful to His Word which He has exalted above His Name (Psalm 138:2). Understanding from His own experiences how difficult it can be to wait patiently on the Lord, the Psalmist gives us these words of encouragement: *"Wait on the Lord: be of good courage, and he shall strengthen thine heart: wait, I say, on the Lord"* (Psalm 27:14, KJV).

So what posture should we assume while we wait? How should the righteous wait for their Father's promises? As I write this, my pastor has been teaching us about walking by faith and not by sight (2 Corinthians 5:7). We are not to be moved by what our circumstances look like but by what God has said about our circumstances. We are reminded that *"the just shall live by faith"* (Habakkuk 2:4, KJV) and that *"without faith it is impossible to please Him..."* (Hebrews 11:6, NKJV). Our diligent seeking after God and our unwavering faith in His faithfulness please Him and that should be our posture before Him.

Therefore, whatever season we find ourselves, we must learn to fight the good fight of faith without relenting. Let us remember that not one Word that our God has spoken will return to Him void. Every Word He has spoken will accomplish the purpose for which it was given (Isaiah 55:11). So, brothers and sisters, know that what may appear to be God's silence is not the case at all. He is at work in us and in our circumstances, from the moment He gives the Word until the time of its fulfillment. What we do in that time of waiting will reveal the difference between waiting with faith or despair.

Pause for reflection: What does waiting on God look like for you? How well do you wait? How might an unwavering stance help you wait better for God's promises to come to pass?

DAY SIX

Perfect love casts out fear

"There is no fear in love. But perfect love drives out fear, because fear has to do with punishment."
(1 John 4:18, NIV)

∞

It was the evening before an important meeting at work and I remembered that my meetings with this particular group of people usually raised feelings of apprehension in me. My discomfort was mostly about the dynamics of our interaction and the negative undertone of our conversations. But then the Holy Spirit brought these words to my remembrance: *"There is no fear in love. But perfect love drives out fear, because fear has to do with punishment. The one who fears is not made perfect in love"* (1 John 4:18, NIV). In a chapter that reminds us to love one another because of the love that God, Himself, has for us, the Holy Spirit directed me to this nugget of truth and reminded me that there is no fear in love. Why should I be afraid when I am a bona fide child of the living God? Behold what manner of love the Father has bestowed on me that I should be called the daughter of God (1 John 3:1).

I immediately thanked God for the peace which came as a result of knowing that I could entrust God with this, too. I was assured that He would give me the right words to say and that He would even direct the meeting Himself. And He did just that. And guess what? I just sat back and watched God do what only He can. He took what could have been a challenging meeting and directed it to the glory of His name. I did not have to fight.

When King Jehoshaphat was facing the invasion of a vast army, we are told that *"the Spirit of the LORD came on Jahaziel son of Zechariah... as he stood in the assembly"* (2 Chronicles 20:14, NIV). And what did God instruct him to tell Jehoshaphat in order to calm his fears?

> *You will not have to fight this battle. Take up your positions; stand firm and see the deliverance the LORD will give you, Judah and Jerusalem. Do not be afraid; do not be discouraged. Go out to face them tomorrow, and the LORD will be with you* (2 Chronicles 20:17, NIV).

Beloved, whatever you are facing today—no matter how small or big it is—just rest in the assurance that God loves you; that He is on your side. And if He is for you, NO ONE can be against you (Romans 8:31) (*emphasis is mine*).

Pause for reflection: What giants are you facing right now? Pray that the Lord opens your eyes to see that He who is for you is bigger than your circumstances. The things you fear cannot withstand His perfect love towards you.

DAY SEVEN

What are you doing here? Get up!

"And he prayed that he might die, and said,
"It is enough! Now, Lord, take my life, for I am no
better than my fathers!"
(1 Kings 19:4, NKJV)

∞

The Scriptures describe the momentary despair which the prophet Elijah faced after a victorious encounter with the prophets of Baal (1 Kings 18). One would imagine that after such a public showdown during which the power and might of God were manifested through him, that Elijah would be operating on a spiritual high. Instead, we learn that he hid in fear when Jezebel demanded that he face the same fate that had befallen the prophets of Baal. Since Elijah was responsible for the death of the prophets of Baal, it was now his turn to fear for his life (1 Kings 19:3).

Did Elijah really believe that Jezebel's might was a match for God's? Hadn't he just asked that the God who answers by fire show Himself to be God? And did God not answer Elijah's prayers by sending down fire to burn up the sacrifice? Yet, here Elijah was, cowering in fear and asking to die. Elijah's despair was brought on by fatigue from the spiritual battle he had just waged and what he was experiencing is not new to humankind. We all go through times when life blindsides us and we are overwhelmed and in despair. Sometimes we do not understand why times of spiritual highs are followed by spiritual lows. We may not speak openly about these things because we are afraid that our faith will be judged by others. Perhaps that is why many of our brothers and sisters suffer alone, ashamed that they feel the way they do.

Are you experiencing despair or hopelessness? Do you feel that you are all alone and that no one cares about you? Do you wonder why the good times don't seem to last or are followed closely behind by difficult times? If your response is "Yes" to any of these questions, you are not alone. We serve a God who is concerned about every aspect of our lives. He sees us at our highs and our lows and His arms are not too short to save us (Isaiah 59:1). When Hagar, Sarai's Egyptian maidservant first ran away from her mistress, she discovered the "God who sees us" −El-Roi (Genesis 16:13). He is still the same God who sees us in all our circumstances today and He has promised to never leave us nor forsake us (Hebrews 13:5). As was the case with Hagar, the angel of God soon came and ministered to Elijah, taking care of his physical needs. Once he had sustenance, he was strengthened in his body and was ready for a private encounter with God. This time God did not announce Himself with pomp and circumstance as He had done in the showdown at Mt. Carmel (1 Kings 18:38). Instead, He came in a still, small voice.

Today, God can come to you in a powerful and spectacular manner or He can come quietly to minister to you. Tune your ear to hear what the Lord is saying to you. In his encounter with the still, quiet voice of God, Elijah was reminded that his work was not over. God still had a purpose for Elijah to accomplish and assured him that he was not the only prophet of God left. The same God wants you to know, today, that your circumstances do not change who He is. Come out from under your circumstances and rise above them in Jesus' name, Amen!

Pause for reflection: When the seasons of your life fluctuate between joy and despair, how can you remain focused on God? How might recalling past victories in Him help when you feel less than victorious?

DAY EIGHT

When the grass IS greener on the other side

*"...for I have learned to be content whatever
the circumstances."*
(Philippians 4:11, NIV)

∞

I am sure you have heard the saying: "The grass always looks greener on the other side." This usually means that someone else might appear to have a better life than we do until we get close enough to them and discover otherwise. We mostly use this phrase to feel better about ourselves when someone else appears to have everything going well for them. We are consoled by the inherent implication that all may not be as well with our neighbor as it seems. To be honest, our assumption that our neighbor may not have such a great life after all may be coming from a place of insecurity and discontentment. Why do we want to minimize what might really be a beautiful life? Could true contentment actually be connected to celebrating what is good in and for others? Today, I am encouraging you, brothers and sisters, to consider that the grass could be greener on the other side. What do you do then?

Paul learned the secret of being content in whatever circumstances he found himself (Philippians 4:11). He had learned to live contentedly with nothing or with everything and he attributed his power to do so to Christ who strengthened him in his weakness. Our source for everything we need, for everything that pertains to life and Godliness is God (2 Peter 1:3). He is the creator and the owner of the earth in all its fullness (Psalm 24:1), and if our earthly fathers, constrained by frail humanity, are able to give us good things, how much more will our Father who owns the cattle on a thousand hills (Matthew 7:11; Psalm 50:10).

Rather than focusing on the health of our neighbor's grass, our attention should be on the faithfulness of our God who has promised to never leave us nor forsake us (Hebrews 13:5). Whether we are in the valley of the shadow of death (Psalm 23:4), or are being threatened by waves of despair that seek to overwhelm us or even destructive fires of life experiences, He has promised to be with us (Isaiah 43:2). So, like Paul, we can say with certainty, that whether we are in want or in plenty, we have learned to be content because everything outside of God is temporal (2 Corinthians 4:18). What will endure is God's everlasting promise of His provision and His presence.

Pause for reflection: Can you see the connection between sharing in the joy of your neighbor's blessings and your state of contentment? How can you cultivate the habit of being happy when good things happen for others?

DAY NINE

Pray using the many names of God
(Pt. 1)

*"The name of the Lord is a strong tower. The
righteous run into it and are safe."*
(Proverbs 18:10, NKJV)

∞

What is in a name? A lot I must say! In most cultures, names
are given after careful consideration of the meaning inherent in
the name. Sometimes, the names we are given are
prophetic. They declare the hopes and dreams that a family
has for their child. At other times, a name can be symbolic
of one's nature and character. In many ways, names are
supposed to announce to others who we are. That is why we
try to live up to the expectations of the names we bear.

In Day Three, I briefly introduced the subject of God's
many names and the ways He lives up to His names when
we seek refuge in Him. Today I will discuss how we can
pray using His names, with the expectancy that He will live
up to His names. In Genesis 1:1, we are introduced to **Elohim**, the
God who is the Three in One, the Creator of all the earth.
The Psalmist proclaims that *"the earth is the Lord's and its
fullness thereof. The world and they that dwell therein"*
(Psalm 24:1, KJV).

So when we are overwhelmed by what appear to be
insurmountable problems of life, all we need to do is
remember that He who hung the stars and the moon and
the sun in the skies and causes the seasons to occur at the
same time every year, is the same God who created us and
knows each one of us by name. Whatever worries we have

pale in comparison to the power of He who spoke the world into existence and owns the cattle on a thousand hills (Psalm 50:10).

In Genesis 17:1, we meet **El–Shaddai**, the all–sufficient God, and the **God Almighty**:

> *When Abram was ninety-nine years old, the LORD appeared to him and said, "I am God Almighty; walk before me faithfully and be blameless* (Genesis 17:1, NKJV).

God declared to him, *"As for Me, behold, My covenant is with you, and you shall be a father of many nations"* (Genesis 17:3, NKJV). Only an Almighty God could make such a covenant with a man who was past his prime. He blessed Abram and his wife with Isaac, the son of promise. Today, God still works mightily on our behalf:

> *For the eyes of the Lord run to and fro throughout the whole earth, to shew himself strong in the behalf of them whose heart is perfect toward him* (2 Chronicles 16:9, KJV).

Whatever your needs are, He is the God who is more than enough for you and your situation.

In Exodus 3:14 (NIV), Moses had a personal encounter with God who appointed him to deliver His people from slavery in Egypt. If Moses were to take the news of deliverance to the Israelites, he needed a name to describe the God who sent him. God said to Moses, *"I AM who I AM. This is what you are to say to the Israelites: 'I AM has sent me to you.'"* Today, God still announces Himself as "**I AM**." He can be who you need Him to be no matter what you are experiencing at the moment, but remember that there is power in recalling and praying using the many names of God.

If we recall who God has revealed Himself to be at various times in His Word, we can pray His Names back to Him. Then we will be encouraged to know that He is *"the same yesterday, today and forever"* (Hebrews 13:8, NIV). If we need help, we can ask the Holy Spirit, and He will call to our remembrance the Names of God for every situation we face. When we are reminded of His past and present faithfulness, we can pray with confidence, knowing that He will always live up to the Names He bears.

Pause for reflection: Are you anxious about anything today? Are you struggling to see beyond your present situation? Ask God to reveal Himself in your circumstances through His many names.

DAY TEN

Pray using the many names of God
(Pt. 2)

Praise the name of God forever and ever, for
he has all wisdom and power
(Daniel 2:20, NLT)

∞

As we continue to encounter God through His many names, we meet Him in Psalm 23, as **Jehovah Raah** or **Jehovah Rohi**, the Lord our Shepherd. Like a shepherd, He guides us away from pitfalls; He provides for our every need. With His rod and His staff, He wards off predators. He refreshes our souls besides the still waters. Our shepherd wants us to be able to discern His voice: *"My sheep hear my voice, and I know them, and they follow me"* (John 10:27, NKJV). Who are you following today and from where do you get your nourishment? Listen for the true Shepherd when He says, *"this is the way, walk in it"* (Isaiah 30:21, NKJV).

Like sheep, we have to stay close to our shepherd because the world around us seems to be in chaos. There are wars and rumors of wars, terrorism, civil unrest, broken homes and broken hearts. But He is **Jehovah Shalom**, the Lord our Peace (1 Thessalonians 5:23; Romans 16:19; Ephesians 2:14). The Bible assures us that God will keep in perfect peace those whose minds are steadfast, because they trust Him (Isaiah 26:3). Our trust is not in our military might. Neither is it in our intellectual might. Yes, some may trust in their horses and chariots (military might and wealth), but we will trust in the name of our God (Psalm 20:7). And if we know Him as Jehovah Shalom, we will not waver, even though the storms of life may rage against us.

When the battle we are facing is sickness in our body or our mind, He is **Jehovah Rapha**, the Lord our Healer. He turned sweet the bitter waters of Marah for the Israelites and there revealed Himself as **Jehovah Rapha** saying:

> *If you listen carefully to the LORD your God and do what is right in His eyes... if you pay attention to His commands and keep all His decrees, I will not bring on you any of the diseases I brought on the Egyptians, for I am the Lord who heals you* (Exodus 15:26, NIV).

Over two thousand years after this proclamation, God made provision for our healing through our Lord Jesus Christ of whom the prophet Isaiah prophesied:

> *But he was pierced for our transgressions, he was crushed for our iniquities; the punishment that brought us peace was on him, and by his wounds we are healed* (Isaiah 53:5, NIV).

This same God reveals Himself as **Jehovah Sabaoth**, the Lord of Hosts. Some translate this to mean the Captain of the Hosts. Can you picture our God leading an army, going forth into battle on our behalf? Remember that the battle is not ours to fight, but the Lord's anyway? (2 Chronicles 20:15)?

What battles are you fighting today? Are you fighting in your own strength? *"This is the Word of the Lord to Zerubbabel: 'Not by might nor by power, but by my Spirit,' says the Lord of Hosts"* (Zechariah 4:6, NKJV). Also the word that Elisha revealed to his servant in the time of battle was: *"Do not fear, for those who are with us are more than those who are with them"* (2 Kings 6:16, NASB). We serve a God who is always ready to do battle on our behalf, so *"Do not be afraid.*

Stand still and see the salvation of the Lord" (Exodus 14:13, NKJV).

It is impossible to do justice here to the many names of our God as they appear in scripture, but I have selected just a few to demonstrate that the weapons of our warfare include remembering and speaking out the names of God into any situation in which we find ourselves. He is the same God today and as He, Himself, has rightly declared, *"I am the Lord and I change not....!"* (Malachi 3:6 KJV).

Pause for reflection: If God Himself has declared His name to be "I AM," then He is inviting you to reflect on the many ways He can move in your circumstances today. Who do you need Him to be today?

DAY ELEVEN

Discovering God's provision in our obedience

"Then Noah built an altar to the LORD and, taking some of all the clean animals and clean birds, he sacrificed burnt offerings on it."
(Genesis 8:20, NIV)

∞

On Day 9, we read that God blessed Abraham with a son in his old age, declaring that through this son, Isaac, Abraham's descendants would be innumerable. God later tested Abraham's faith when He asked him to sacrifice the son of promise. We are familiar with the story of Abraham's obedience and his later discovery of God's faithfulness. Just as Abraham was about to kill Isaac, he discovered that God had already made provision for the sacrifice by placing a ram in the thicket. God had revealed Himself as Jehovah Jireh, the Lord God who provides. Now, let us consider the similarity to the story of Noah's obedience to God. The Bible tells us that *"Noah was a righteous man, blameless among the people of his time, and he walked faithfully with God"* (Genesis 6:9, NIV).

The Lord saw how great the wickedness of the human race had become on the earth, and that every inclination of the thoughts of the human heart was only evil all the time. The Lord regretted that he had made human beings on the earth, and his heart was deeply troubled. So the Lord said, "I will wipe from the face of the earth the human race I have created—and with them the animals, the birds and the creatures that move along the ground—for I regret that I have made them." But Noah found favor in the eyes of the Lord (Genesis 6:5-8, NIV).

Because Noah pleased God, God saved Noah and his family from destruction. But God had some instructions for Noah and we are told that, *"Noah did everything just as God commanded him"* (Genesis 6:22, NIV). Just like Abraham after him, Noah obeyed God. He took the clean and unclean animals into the ark as God required. When we first read this, the purpose of preserving the animals for future procreation is apparent in these commands:

Take with you seven pairs of every kind of clean animal, a male and its mate, and one pair of every kind of unclean animal, a male and its mate, and also seven pairs of every kind of bird, male and female, to keep their various kinds alive throughout the earth (Genesis 7:2-3, NIV).

What is not initially obvious is another purpose for the preservation of the clean animals. But when the flood waters had receded, *"Noah built an altar to the LORD and, taking some of all the clean animals and clean birds, he sacrificed burnt offerings on it"* (Genesis 8:20, NIV). When the flood was over, the first thing Noah did was to offer thanks and praise to God. God smelled the sweet aroma of Noah's sacrifice and He was pleased. You see, God made provision for the sacrifice ahead of time when He asked Noah to preserve some clean animals in the ark. And Noah's obedience made room for the revelation of God's provision and faithfulness.

The place of ultimate sacrifice to God is in the moment we say "Yes" and yield our will to Him. It is only a matter of time before He reveals that, in the act of our obedience, He has already made provision for us.

Pause for reflection: Is there anything you feel God tugging at you to surrender? What is stopping you from believing that, for every sacrifice, He has already made provision?

DAY TWELVE

When God's answer to prayer is "My grace is sufficient"

"My grace is sufficient for you, for my power is made perfect in weakness."
(2 Corinthians 12:9, NIV)

∞

One night, the Spirit of the Lord deposited a metaphor into my spirit which meaning I immediately understood. What I heard in my spirit was that I could withdraw from God's account amounts that far exceed what I have deposited. I continued to meditate on this all night. The next morning, I was reminded of Paul's conversation with God concerning the thorn in his flesh, the agent of Satan, which God allowed in Paul's life to keep him grounded and not boastful of the revelations of heaven which he had received. Three times Paul prayed to God to remove the thorn in his flesh and three times God answered him: *"My grace is sufficient for you, for my power is made perfect in weakness"* (2 Corinthians 12:9, NIV) *(emphasis is mine)*.

This is my understanding of God's response to Paul's prayer:

> *I will not remove the thorn, for it is there to serve a purpose. This will not kill you, for I will be with you as you walk with the thorn. My grace will be more than enough to get you through. Even in your weakness, my strength will make you strong.*

It occurred to me that the Word I had received the night before was directing me towards God's grace. It was reminding me of the blessing of withdrawing grace (unmerited favor) from God's account in amounts that I can never pay back. As Paul reminds us:

God raised us up with Christ and seated us with him in the heavenly realms in Christ Jesus, in order that in the coming ages he might show the incomparable riches of his grace, expressed in his kindness to us in Christ Jesus. For it is by grace you have been saved, through faith—and this is not from yourselves, it is the gift of God—not by works, so that no one can boast (Ephesians 2:6-9, NIV).

Just as Paul could not boast of the things that had been revealed to him by God, we cannot boast about earning God's saving and keeping grace by our works. Our righteousness is like filthy rags before God's holiness and without His saving grace we cannot stand before a Holy God (Isaiah 64:6). Thank you, Father, for your strength which girds us up when we are weak, and thank you for your grace which is fresh each new day. Thank you for the reminder that we can never out give you. We can rest only in the knowledge that all that we will ever need is found in abundant in you.

Pause for reflection: Do you ever feel that you are not good enough to be so loved and forgiven by a righteous God? You are correct, you are not! But His grace is more than we will ever need. Do not ever doubt the sufficiency of His grace!

DAY THIRTEEN

God's everlasting covenant through the generations

"As for me, this is my covenant with them,"
says the Lord. "My Spirit... will not depart from
you, and my words that I have put in your mouth
will always be on your lips, on the lips of your
children and on the lips of their descendants—
from this time on and forever," says the Lord.
(Isaiah 59:21, NIV)

∞

Our God is a generational God. He is not limited to our own concepts of time and space. He is not just concerned about us, but He is also concerned about our future generations. God required of Abram to leave all that was familiar and dear to him and separate himself to a land that God had prepared for him and his descendants. In return for his obedience, God promised to bless Abram's future generations even while He vowed to make them as countless as the stars in the sky and the sand on the seashore (Genesis 12:3).

God changed Abram's name to Abraham as a confirmation of how much He would enlarge his territory. He made an everlasting covenant between Himself, Abraham and Abraham's descendants, vowing to be his God and the God of Abraham's descendants after him (Genesis 17: 6-7). His promises to Abraham are an example of the eternal reach of God's wisdom and influence. Even when the circumstances around us do not match what the Spirit of God is saying to us, we should remember that He does not lie. If He has made a promise, He will keep it.

As believers, we desire for our household to be saved and walking faithfully after God, but we may not always have the perfect scenario where an entire household is equally yoked in their faith. They may appear like oxen pulling in different directions, and it may seem like our prayers for the salvation of our loved ones are ineffectual and futile. Paul offers some comfort in these words:

> *For the unbelieving husband has been sanctified through his wife, and the unbelieving wife has been sanctified through her believing husband. Otherwise your children would be unclean, but as it is, they are holy* (1 Corinthians 7:14, NIV).

Does this imply that our family members do not have to seek a relationship with God through Christ for themselves? Of course not! We are only assured that once the Spirit of the Living God is welcomed into a home, it is just a matter of time before God's promises come true, before the words He has put in our mouths be forever on our lips, on the lips of our children and the lips of their descendants (Isaiah 59:21).

God's promises toward us are not limited to our generation. He has promised to lavish unfailing love for a thousand generations on those who love [Him] and obey [His] commands (Exodus 20:6). Speaking to the children of Israel about His jealousy for their faithfulness to Him and Him only, God also speaks of visiting the fathers' iniquity on the third and fourth generation (Exodus 20:5). So whether for good or bad, God's dealings with His people transcend the current generation. Therefore, if you are believing God for the salvation of your loved ones, stay steadfast and continue to trust that your household will be saved.

Pause for reflection: How would you believe differently and how would you live your life differently knowing that God's judgment and lovingkindness extend to your future generations?

DAY FOURTEEN

When the call of the world distracts us
from the call of God

*"But Jesus often withdrew to lonely places
and prayed."*
(Luke 5:16, NIV)

∞

I see it everywhere I go. It is tucked inside the side of the head scarves elegantly wrapped around the women's heads and in the earpieces that have now become a fashion statement. It is in the hands of the toddler whose mother needs a moment of quiet and the reason for the driver in front of me swerving briefly off the road. Technology has become the bane of our existence. We are clutching on for dear life to one gadget or the other; our faces are perpetually buried in any one of them. We miss the frown on our neighbor's face and hardly hear the sighs of despair around us. Even when the Holy Spirit tugs at our spirit, asking us to come away with Him for a moment, we wrestle with detaching from the world around us, even as our hearts long for the days of much prayer and worship.

Where are the days of walking with God in the cool of the day like Adam did? And the days of sitting close enough to hear His heartbeat? What about the quiet of morning meditations and night seasons of sweet communion? The Psalmist says, *"In the morning, Lord, you hear my voice; in the morning I lay my requests before you and wait expectantly"* (Psalm 5:3, NIV). Even Jesus taught us by example. He often went away from the crowd to spend time with God. The Son of God needed the regular refreshing which comes from communing with the Father. Even on one such occasion His disciples wanted what He had. They asked Him to teach them to pray.

What is distracting you from spending time with God? He is waiting for you just as He has promised. If we draw near to Him, He will draw near to us (James 4:8). He also said, *"Call to me and I will answer and tell you great and unsearchable things you do not know"* (Jeremiah 33:3, NIV). In another place, He promised that we will call upon Him and come and pray to Him, and He will listen to us (Jeremiah 29:12). He declares that we will seek Him and find Him when we seek Him with all our heart. He promises that we WILL find Him (Jeremiah 29: 12-14) (*emphasis is mine*).

Today, if you hear His voice, do not harden your hearts or be hard of hearing (Psalm 95: 8). The next time you feel God tugging at your heart, steal away to hear what He has to say. And sometimes, words are not necessary. He just wants to hold you close.

Pause for reflection: Where do you go or to what or whom do you turn to quench the restlessness that sometimes creeps in when we stray from God? How might detaching yourself from the world and spending time with God quiet your soul?

DAY FIFTEEN

The love walk: walking the talk

"By this shall all men know that ye are my disciples, if
ye have love one to another."
(John 13:35, KJV)

"This is my commandment, that ye love one another, as I
have loved you."
(John 15:12, KJV)

∞

I noticed there was something different about my neighbor. She had lost her hair and now wore a baseball cap every time I saw her. My family's first thought was the dreaded word, "cancer." We even speculated that she may have donated her hair for a good cause. But we did not have the courage to ask. After all, everyone in my neighborhood kept to themselves, except for the occasional wave. Then my husband broke the ice. He stopped and talked with her one day while he was walking back from the mail box. She confirmed our fears. She had cancer and had been undergoing treatment for a few months. And my heart broke for her and for what it must have been like to get the news that no one wants to hear. I went out the next day and got her a potted plant and a card. I did not want to get flowers that would wither in a few days.

As I stepped over the threshold of her home for a visit, I was reminded of how we have been commanded to love one another as Jesus Christ has loved us (John 15:12). How has He loved us? Unconditionally! Without Christ, we love conditionally. The social messages we hear are, "As long as you are good to me, I will love you" or "If you reach out first, then I will respond." These are the mindsets that keep the walls up between neighbors.

An expert in the law asked Jesus, "Who is my neighbor?" (Luke 10:25). And Jesus assured the man that he already knew the answer. After all, he was well versed in the Law. The man knew about the commandment to not only love God, but to love his neighbor as he loved himself (Deuteronomy 6:5; Leviticus 19:18). But it was not enough to know; he had to practice it like the good Samaritan in the parable of the good neighbor (Luke 10:25-37).

So I apologized to my neighbor that it took the news of the cancer for me to visit her after almost five years of our just making polite talk. All I wanted to do was love and support her and I made sure she understood that. As she walked me out, we noticed that it had rained in the time I had been visiting with her. We had been unaware of this, and I was reminded of how often we are unaware of what is happening behind the scenes of other's lives while we go about our daily affairs.

Has the Holy Spirit been tugging at your heart to reach out to a friend, neighbor or co-worker? What is stopping you? Remember that we cannot love our neighbors as ourselves if we do not first reach out to them. Citing from the Old Testament, Jesus commands:

> *And you shall love the Lord your God with all your heart, with all your soul, with all your mind, and with all your strength. This is the first commandment. And the second, like it, is this: 'You shall love your neighbor as yourself.' There is no other commandment greater than these* (Mark 12:30-31, NKJV).

Many times we focus on the first commandment to love God and neglect the second, to love our neighbor, but God cautions that He *"desires mercy and not sacrifice, and the knowledge of God more than burnt offerings"* (Hosea 6:6, NKJV). Loving our neighbors and showing them mercy should be a natural outcome of loving God first. So, go forth and be merciful to someone today. Sometimes that is all it takes to extend God's love to others.

Pause for reflection: Who has the Lord laid on your heart today? Do you need to extend love to anyone? What is stopping you?

DAY SIXTEEN

Aligning our will to God's: the Gethsemane example

"Abba, Father, everything is possible for you. Take this cup from me. Yet, not what I will, but what you will."
(Mark 14:36, NIV)

∞

The story of Jesus' travail in the garden of Gethsemane allows us a glimpse into His humanity. The time for Him to take upon Himself the sins of humankind and endure a momentary separation from God was nigh. Matthew describes the sorrow that came upon Jesus, saying He was *"overwhelmed with sorrow to the point of death"* (Matthew 26:38, NIV). He fell on His face in earnest intercession which caused sweat like drops of blood to appear on Him (Luke 22:44). In other words, Jesus felt very human feelings like you and I have felt or are going to feel at some point in our lives.

The Bible reminds us that *"we do not have a High Priest who cannot sympathize with our weaknesses, but was in all points tempted as we are, yet without sin"* (Hebrews 4:15, NKJV). Jesus experienced loneliness when His friends could not keep watch with Him in Gethsemane. He was tired from rejection, persecution, and spiritual travail and wanted it all to end. He experienced discouragement and, twice, He pleaded that the cup of suffering be taken away from Him, but twice He surrendered to God's will concerning His impending death. The Bible does not capture the duration of His suffering in Gethsemane. It may have been minutes or hours, but Jesus came to a place of surrender: *"Abba, Father, everything is possible for you.*

Take this cup from me. Yet, not what I will, but what you will." (Mark 14:36, NIV)

Do you sometimes feel that the ordeal you are going through is new and has never being experienced by others? Do you ever feel that God has abandoned you in your suffering? You, too, can surrender like Jesus did. Then you are able to align your will to God's and are able to say like Jesus did, "YET, not what I will, but what you will" (*emphasis is mine*). Our surrender is always in the YET. Jesus *"learned obedience from what he suffered and, once made perfect, he became the source of eternal salvation for all who obey him"* (Hebrews 5:8-9, NIV). How did He learn obedience? By submitting to the will of God. May we, too, learn obedience from what we suffer and yield to God's will for all aspects of our lives.

Pause for reflection: What is going on in your life presently that would cause you to despair? Are you able to surrender with the response, "yet, not my will, but yours be done, Oh God?"

DAY SEVENTEEN

What is the attention span of your offense?

"It is impossible that no offenses should come."
(Luke 17:1, NKJV)

∞

How long do you hold on to an offense? Do you feel justified in holding on to some grudges? Do you know that offenses are a natural consequence of human interaction? Even Jesus assured His disciples:

> *It is impossible that no offenses should come...take heed to yourselves. If your brother sins against you, rebuke him; and if he repents, forgive him. And if he sins against you seven times in a day, and seven times in a day returns to you saying, 'I repent,' you shall forgive him... And the apostles said to the Lord, 'Increase our faith'* (Luke 17:1-5, NKJV).

How much faith do I need to forgive my brother or sister over and over again? More faith than I already have? That is what the disciples seemed to ponder when they asked Jesus to increase their faith. It is interesting that the disciples made the connection between faith and forgiveness. We need faith in order to forgive others when they offend us.

Matthew's epistle recounts a similar conversation between Peter and Jesus on the subject of forgiveness. Peter wanted to know the term limit on the number of times he had to forgive his brother. He threw out the number "seven" expecting that to be impressive, but Jesus took Peter's attention off his victim mentality and turned it towards the notion that we who have been forgiven much should be willing to forgive much (Matthew 18:21-35). Jesus challenged Peter to extend forgiveness "seventy times seven," not as the magic number of times to forgive one another but to teach him that there are no term limits with grace. And elsewhere Jesus says:

> *For if you forgive men their trespasses, your heavenly Father will also forgive you. But if you do not forgive men their trespasses, neither will your Father forgive your trespasses* (Matthew 6:14-15, NKJV).

Jesus assures us of several things in the Bible. He assures us that we WILL have trials in this world, but He does not leave us hopeless (John 10:10) (*emphasis is mine*). He also assures us that we will overcome because He has overcome (John 10:10). In today's reading, He gives us another assurance–that there will be plenty of opportunities in our daily lives to be offended. Although this is so, how we respond is important. Our reaction to offense may seem justifiable, but most times it only makes the situation worse.

You may ask again, "Why should I forgive?" When we feel that we have been victimized, we desire revenge over forgiveness. And even when we choose to forgive, we expect God to reward us for our obedience. But Jesus reminds us that our response to God's command to forgive is our duty to Him (Luke 17:10). And what does Solomon say is the whole duty of man? It is to fear God and to keep His commandments because He will judge every good and evil thing we have done (Ecclesiastes 12:13-14). If this is not enough reason to forgive those who offend us, I don't know what else is!

Pause for reflection: So, how long do you hold on to your offense? Who do you need to forgive today? What is stopping you?

DAY EIGHTEEN

What thoughts does God think towards us?

"For I know the thoughts that I think toward
you, saith the Lord, thoughts of peace, and not of
evil, to give you an expected end."
(Jeremiah 29:11, KJV)

∞

It was not until I started to write this particular devotion that I realized that the words "thoughts" and "plans" are used interchangeably in the above quote depending on the Bible translation one is using. It means that for God to have plans for His people, He is thinking about them. God does not forget His children, no matter what we might think at times. There are some examples of God's remembrance in the Bible. For example, He remembered Noah after the flood waters had covered the earth for 150 days and after everything that was not safe in the ark had died. He caused the flood waters to recede (Genesis 8:1). Another instance is the story of Rachel whose father, Laban, cheated her out of her rightful place as Jacob's first wife. Although her sister was blessed with many sons, she endured barrenness; yet, God remembered her and gave her a son, Joseph (Genesis 30:22).

Joseph's birth and life are significant in the way they demonstrate God's thoughts towards us and His remembrance of His people. Although he was despised by his brothers and sold into slavery, Joseph later became the second in command to Pharaoh, King of Egypt, and provided a way for his family to migrate to Egypt during a great famine. With time, Joseph, his brothers and their generation died in Egypt and there arose a new king who knew nothing about Joseph and his influence in Egypt. He became jealous of the Israelites who continued to increase in number and become a military threat and enslaved them. After their many years of enduring the burden of slavery, God remembered His covenant with Abraham, Isaac and Jacob and intervened on behalf of the Israelites in Egypt (Exodus: 2:24). He raised a deliverer in Moses.

In today's Bible verse, the children of Israel have been in exile in Babylon, but God remembered them and sent words of encouragement to them through the prophet, Jeremiah. He assured them that it was okay to settle down, marry and be engaged in their place of exile. Even though they would be in Babylon for seventy years, He would remember them and come to them to fulfill the plans that He had for them. The thoughts and plans that He had towards them spoke of a future hope. It was a future that would bring an end to their captivity in Babylon—a future where they would call upon Him and He would listen. He would restore their fortunes and bring them back to their homeland.

God thinks about us and He remembers us. He thinks good thoughts towards us. When we have endured years of captivity to our circumstances and it looks like God has forgotten us, we should look back at His track record and recall that He is El–Roi, the God who sees (Genesis 16:13) and He will never forsake us (Hebrews 13:5).

Pause for reflection: Are you facing difficulties in your life right now and do you feel that God has forgotten you? Be encouraged and remember that He is true to His promise. He will remember you because He thinks about you.

DAY NINETEEN

The pebble in David's hand

"The race is not to the swift or the battle to the strong... but time and chance happen to them all."
(Ecclesiastes 9:11, NKJV)

∞

Contrary to popular belief, the best man or woman does not always win. Today's Bible verse shows that speed and strength do not always guarantee a win. It is God's timing and favor that determine the victor. God has chosen the foolish things of the world to confound the wise and the weak things of the world to confound the strong. He has even chosen the good-for-nothing, the despised, to bring to nothing the things that are highly esteemed by the world. And why has He done all these things? So that neither the weak nor the strong, the foolish nor the wise nor the despised will boast in anyone else but God (1 Corinthians 1:27).

An illustration of how God can use the inconsequential and insignificant things of the world to accomplish His purposes is found in the story of David's defeat of Goliath. For the purposes of today's devotion, I will shift our attention from David's size and might in comparison to Goliath's and focus on the pebble in David's sling. We know the story of David's selection of the five pebbles for his fight against Goliath and about the one which brought the giant down. If the pebble could speak, I imagine that it may have perceived itself to be inconsequential in size and function compared to perhaps the large boulders around it. Yet, that one pebble was all it took to kill Goliath. God's favor was not only on David but on the means by which the giant was brought down.

The strength of just one pebble in David's hand reminds us that God is no respecter of the means by which He carries out His purposes. Just as He supernaturally enabled a young shepherd boy to bring down a much feared giant with an insignificant weapon, He delights in being our strength when we are weak (2 Corinthians 12:9). So, the next time you face giants in your life, don't try to fight them in your own strength. Remember that God's power, grace and favor will empower you to achieve far more than you can on your own. This is what Paul meant when he declared: *"Be strong in the Lord and in the power of his might"* (Ephesians 6:10, KJV).

Pause for reflection: Have you ever doubted your ability to fulfill God's assignments? Remember that God's weakness is stronger than the greatest of human strength. The pebble in David's hand had no might of its own, but the power of God in David was mightier.

DAY TWENTY

Jesus our Ebenezer

*"When my heart is overwhelmed, lead me to
the rock that is higher than I."*
(Psalm 61:2, KJV)

∞

In recent times, we have been plagued by various natural disasters. From tornadoes and floods to drought and wildfire, we are reminded regularly that we are living in a time when our lives can literally change in a twinkling of an eye. The week I was writing this devotion, many watched in amazement as a road in Baltimore, Maryland, gave way and as the cars parked alongside it tumbled onto the railroad tracks beneath. The rains had been quite heavy and the resulting floods caused the road to give way. The cars fell in one swoop as if they had been swallowed by the earth beneath them.

Natural disasters are not the only problems that people encounter today. All around us people are hurting—we all know people who are struggling with unemployment, illness, divorce, infertility, loss of a loved one, etc. Even some of us are experiencing these struggles ourselves. Although it seems like there is so much despair around us, we must not lose hope because we are not a people who do not know their God. At one of his lowest moments, King David penned Psalm 61: 1-4 (KJV):

*Hear my cry, O God; attend unto my prayer.
From the end of the earth will I cry unto you,
when my heart is overwhelmed: lead me to the
rock that is higher than I. For thou has been a*

shelter for me, and a strong tower from the enemy.

In David's cry, it was apparent to whom he turned when his heart was overwhelmed. We all have been in that place where it seems like we are consumed by the despair and hopelessness around us. We have felt as if the ground under our feet is unstable. Whether we are hard-pressed on every side physically or spiritually, we have a Rock that is higher than we are. His name is Jesus. He is our Ebenezer—our Rock (1 Samuel 7:12). He teaches us about the importance of building our house on solid rock so that when the storms of life come, and we are buffeted on every side, we are able to stand because our feet are firmly planted in Him (Matthew 7:24-27). As the old hymn reminds us:

On Christ the solid rock [we] stand, ALL other ground is sinking sand (emphasis is mine).

So brethren, let us not be like the foolish man who builds his house on an unstable foundation. He does not build in preparation for the storms that will surely come. For as Jesus Himself has reminded us, trials and tribulations will come, but Jesus has triumphed over them; therefore, we too have overcome (John 16:33). We may sway from the pressures of storms and we may be shaken, but if we are firmly rooted in Him, we will survive. Like Paul, we can declare:

We are troubled on every side, yet not distressed; we are perplexed, but not in despair; persecuted, but not forsaken; cast down but not destroyed...
(2 Corinthians 4:8-9, KJV).

Take heart, brothers and sisters, and let not your hearts be troubled in these times (John 14:1)! We know whose we are and He has promised to be with us till the end of the age (Matthew 28:20).

Pause for reflection: On what foundation do you build your life? Are you experiencing any storms in your life right now? Remember that the God who speaks to the storms, the one whom the waves and the winds obey, has you safe in the palm of His hands. Build on this!

DAY TWENTY-ONE

The deceitful heart

"Keep your heart with all diligence, for out of
it spring the issues of life."
(Proverbs 4:23, NKJV)

∞

In December 2000, I was going through a time of deep hurt like I had never felt before that time. I had been misunderstood and lied about. I could not defend myself because my accusers had made up their minds about me. Little did I know that times of still more hurt were around the corner, but my Father in heaven knew. I had been experiencing divine visitations in the night season and I had learned to recognize these as times to be still so I could hear from Him. Only He knew the purpose that these visitations would later serve.

One night, I had just returned from driving three hours each way to pick up my sister and her family who were visiting for the holidays. Naturally I was tired from the drive and the preparation for their visit. But the Lord visited me that night and spoke these words to my spirit: *"Keep your heart with all diligence, for out of it spring the issues of life"* (Proverbs 4:23, NKJV). I knew immediately to what He was referring. I was still struggling to come to terms with the way I had been treated, but God was asking me to trust Him. It was not that it did not matter to Him that I had been treated unfairly, but He knew that what would count in the end would be the condition of my heart.

When more times of betrayal and hurt followed, I did not struggle with bitterness or resentment because God had already warned me about keeping my heart pure. At night, I would fall asleep with praise and worship songs on my lips. In the day, I held on for dear life to the Word of God. I continued to think loving thoughts and act lovingly towards my accusers, even in the face of their continued rejection.

Why did God warn me about taking stock of the condition of my heart? Speaking through Jeremiah, He said:

> *The heart is deceitful above all things, and desperately wicked: who can know it? I the Lord search the heart, I try the reins, even to give every man according to his ways, and according to the fruit of his doings* (Jeremiah 17: 9-10, KJV).

We can manage to fool others, but *"the spirit of man is the candle of the Lord, searching all the inward parts of the belly"* (Proverbs 20:27, KJV). God was more concerned about the state of the health of my heart than the lies that had been spoken about me because He wants to be able to embrace me one day and welcome me home as a good and faithful servant. He wants to be able to acknowledge that I was faithful over these things that happened along life's way. He has promised that at that time, He will make me ruler over many things. Then I will enter into the joy of the Lord (Matthew 25:21).

Pause for reflection: When you think over the course of your life, can you remember times of betrayal and pain? How did you handle them? Did you depend on God's help to walk away from bitterness or resentment or did you feel justified? What do you think God requires of you?

DAY TWENTY-TWO

Desperate faith

"If I may but touch his garment, I shall be whole."
(Matthew. 9:21, KJV)

∞

She is known only as the woman with the issue of blood. We do not know her real name. All we know is that she had been bleeding for 12 years and had exhausted all her resources, after baffling all the physicians she consulted. Her identity was now solely based on the issue with which she was struggling. Sometimes we take on the identity of our struggles and become known mainly by that thorn in our side which the Lord does not seem in a hurry to remove. This woman's story is one of desperation.

If you have known what it is to be in a desperate place where every human solution to your problem has failed, then you may also identify with the shameless courage which caused her to defy the religious restrictions of her time. According to the laws of her time, she was ceremoniously unclean, which meant that she was forced to isolate herself from others. There is nothing more depressing than to feel that you are all alone in your struggle or that you have been shunned for something that is not of your own creation. Had she watched from her solitary confinement at the crowd that thronged the man of Galilee and determined in her heart to get to Him someday? Sometimes when we have waited so long for our miracle, a surge of desperate faith is all we need to believe for our deliverance.

In her desperation she joined the crowd which followed after Jesus that day. She was probably bowed from years of cowering in shame and neglect, but this very posture granted her access to the hem of Jesus's gown. As soon as she made the connection and touched the fringes of His gown, her desperate faith drew on the anointing which Christ, the Anointed One, carried. And He knew it! He knew that someone had made a desperate connection to Him and He had to stop to identify who it was. We can imagine the mix of fear and wonder she felt as she realized that, in her defiance of the law, she had been made whole again. She had attracted the Master's attention and He publicly acknowledged her faith and asked her to depart in peace.

How she must have held her head high now as she returned home, knowing that one encounter with Jesus had forever changed her life. Her faith had made her whole. Remember, today, that all you need is just enough faith in Christ, the Anointed one and you, too, will be able to draw from the anointing that destroys every yoke.

Pause for reflection: Have you ever been so desperate for a touch from God that you knew you would not make it without His help? If so, what did you do? If this is where you are right now, know that all you need is found in Him alone. He is waiting for you.

DAY TWENTY-THREE

Finding God in an ordinary day

"Let us then approach God's throne of grace with confidence, so that we may receive mercy and find grace to help us in our time of need."
(Hebrews 4:16, NIV)

∞

This is what finding God in the midst of an ordinary day looked like to me one day. My daughter marched into the kitchen, plopped a jar of my body cream on the kitchen counter and proceeded to apply it onto her arms and elbows. I pointed out to her that the cream was mine, and that I had noticed the boldness with which she took it without my permission. She did not try to hide the fact that she was using my cream but rather stood boldly in front of me as she applied it.

I was immediately reminded that this is how God wants us to approach Him—boldly and without fear like His children. My daughter rightly assumed that I would have no problem with her using something which belonged to me. In fact, she was so confident that she did not sneak around to use it. Even when I pointed out that it was mine, she just smiled and kept at the task of applying the cream. That is the type of confidence God our Father wants us to have in Him. My daughter did not think, "Maybe my mom is still mad at me for something I did, and I wonder if I am worthy enough to use her cream?" Sometimes we hold on to the memories of past sins which God has already forgiven and disqualify ourselves from boldly approaching Him. My daughter walked in the strong assurance that I loved her and wanted the best for her and that whatever I owned was available to her.

God has instructed us to ask, seek and knock (Matt. 7:7). He desires to give us what we need even to a greater extent than our earthly family. He wants us to approach Him with unwavering faith, believing that that if the Word says that He loves us with an everlasting love, then it is true (Jeremiah 31:3). We should, therefore, approach God's throne of grace with confidence (Hebrews 4:16).

So, today, let us repent of our double-minded ways and for limiting the power of His Word to do what He said it would do. Let us remember that God's ways and thoughts are not like our ways and thoughts and that His Word accomplishes everything He said it would (Isaiah 55:8;11). The next time you are hesitant to boldly ask and receive from your heavenly Father, remember that a double-minded man or woman appears to be unstable and will not obtain favor from God (James 1: 6-7).

Pause for reflection: What holds you back from approaching God with boldness in your time of need? Do you measure God's love for you by the way your earthly family extends love toward you?

DAY TWENTY-FOUR

The living Word of God

*"The teaching of your Word gives light, so
even the simple can understand."*
(Psalm 119:130)

∞

Sometimes I find that worry about various situations can begin to slowly creep into my thoughts and easily consume my day. If I am not careful to take these thoughts captive and bring them under the subjection of Christ and the Word of God (2 Corinthians 10:5), I can quickly find myself becoming overwhelmed by negative thoughts that do not line up with the truth of God's Word. When I turn to the Word of God, I have discovered the truth in the Psalmist's words that the unfolding of [God's] Word gives light and gives understanding to the simple [me] (Psalm 119:130). How does the Word of God bring insight and change? – through reading and meditating on the Word. The Psalmist concludes, *"I have hidden your Word in my heart that I might not sin against you"* (Psalm 119:11, NLT).

When I worry about my circumstances, real and imagined, I am sinning against God because I am making Him out to be a liar. His promises towards me are many and they are true. I have to call them up from the places where I have hidden them in my heart. I remember that He has promised to never leave me nor forsake me (Hebrews 13:5). He has said that He will be with me till the end of the age (Matthew 28:20). In Jeremiah 33:3, He promises that if I call upon Him, that He will answer and show me great and mighty things that I know not of. Elsewhere I have read that His eyes search to and fro the earth, looking to show Himself strong on behalf of those whose hearts are committed to Him (2 Chronicles 16:9).

Without fail, whenever I have taken the time to turn to His Word–not someone else's interpretation of what He says but His actual living Word, I have experienced Him all anew as the burden lifter. I have encountered His anointing which breaks every yoke (Isaiah 10:27). I have learned all over again that I should cast my care upon Him for He cares for me (1 Peter 5:7) When I am weary and heavily burdened from trying to carry my cares myself, He beckons me to come to Him, heavy burden and all, and to cast my cares on Him. And because He cares for me, the rest that He gives is enduring (Matthew 11:28).

God's Word is forever settled in heaven (Psalm 119:89). When I take the negative thoughts which the enemy, the eternal liar, is feeding into my mind and I replace them with the truth of God's Word; when I dwell on whatsoever things are true, honest, just, pure, lovely, of good report, things that are virtuous and praiseworthy (Philippians 4:8); then, the peace of God which passes all understanding surely comes (Philippians 4:7). It may not come right away, but it does come. Then I am able to experience the light that comes from the entrance of His Word into my spirit. I am strengthened in my inner man and I can say I am strong (Joel 3:10); I am redeemed (Psalm 107:2); I am the apple of God's eye (Zechariah 2:8), and I will no longer be burdened by the yoke of worry because I know that my redeemer lives (Job 19:25).

Pause for reflection: What is that thing that keeps you bound in constant worry and unrest? Hand it over to the lover of your soul and leave it in His hands. He is much more able than you are to carry your burdens.

DAY TWENTY-FIVE

Lavish love: loving your neighbor as yourself

"Blessed are the peacemakers for they will be
called sons of God."
(Matthew 5:9, NIV)

∞

In teaching His disciples about loving their enemies, Jesus emphasized the futility of retaliating when they were wronged. Although the teachings of the Law called for retributive justice, *"Eye for eye, tooth for tooth ..."* (Exodus 21:24, NIV), Jesus challenged them to love their enemies and pray for those who persecute them (Matthew 5:44). Jesus was inspiring them to go against the grain and be peacemakers. They were not to be like the rest of the world whose natural instinct is to repay evil with evil and good with good. Earlier, He had taught them, *"Blessed are the peacemakers for they will be called sons of God"* (Matthew 5:9, NIV). If you often find yourself in the peace-making role, do not be discouraged. You have been called to a world that is full of darkness, and you cannot win others over by repaying evil with evil.

Thousands of years ago, King Solomon instructed:

If your enemy is hungry, give him bread to eat; and if he is thirsty, give him water to drink; for so you will heap coals of fire on his head, and the Lord will reward you (Proverbs 25:21-22, NIV).

Jesus was asking His followers at that time and future disciples (us) to have the mind of Christ concerning our fellow human beings. If God, who sees the condition of all hearts, causes the sun to rise and the rain to fall on both the just and the unjust, then He is able to help us have the mind of Christ towards others. God will not reward us for loving only those who first love us. According to Jesus, the heathen and sinners do that very well. If we seek the way of peace, we are the children of God, and if we are His children, then He is more than able to assist us in our walk with Him. When we find it difficult to walk in love toward others, all we have to do is ask of Him who is perfect, who loved us even when we did not love Him, and He will give us the wisdom and strength to do that which is difficult. After all, He *"gives generously to all without finding fault"* (James 1:5, NIV).

The futility of a life that is not hidden with Christ in God is demonstrated in the lives of those who choose hate, instead of love; vengeance in the place of forgiveness and bitterness instead of joy (Colossians 3:3). We are not called to love as the world does, but we are to give love, grace and mercy as freely as we have received them. As Jesus reminds us, *"Freely you have received; freely give"* (Matthew 10:8, NKJV). The command is still relevant today to those of us who daily drink from the fountain of God's goodness and mercy which follows us all the days of our lives (Psalm 23:6).

Pause for reflection: Paul advises us not to conform to the world's thinking patterns but to imitate Jesus in the way we relate to others. You can love others lavishly if you always remember that God first loved us lavishly.

DAY TWENTY-SIX

Spiritual fast-food or wholesome food for thought

"For as he thinks in his heart, so is he..."
(Proverbs 23:7a, NKJV)

∞

Our society is the most health conscious it has ever been. Our nutritional preferences now range from fat-free and sugar-free, to gluten-free and non-GMO. Most people are aware that a fast food diet will clog your arteries in due time; therefore, many are opting for food that is clean, fresh, locally-grown, organic or sourced from Community Supported Agriculture (CSA) farms. We are diligent with reading labels and measuring and weighing food portions. But what about spiritual fast food and applying due diligence to what we allow into our minds? Wouldn't it make sense to assume that what we ingest spiritually can lead to the clogging of our spiritual senses?

I heard the words "spiritual fast food" while I was praying one morning and I knew exactly what the Lord was saying to me. He was asking me to consider the junk that I allow into my mind. We are bombarded daily by media messages that affect the way we think about ourselves and others. The media sets the agenda of what enters through our eye-gates and ear-gates. If we are not careful, we may end up confused and conflicted about our true values and the values that the world wants us to adopt as our own.

We don't want to be passive thinkers who just allow any thought to wander through and make its home in our minds. Before long, these thoughts start to seep into our conversations, behaviors and interactions with others. If we think too long that the entire world is against us, then we soon begin to believe this and project it on to others. If we analyze a casual conversation too closely, we are bound to read into it meanings that are not intended and react accordingly. If we constantly hear that we need one more product, one more toy to make us valuable in the eyes of others, we will begin to think that we are undeserving of unconditional love and acceptance. That is what the wise man means when he proclaims that we are what we think (Proverbs 23:7).

Paul cautions us to beware of the thoughts which occupy our minds. We should make a practice of evaluating them accordingly: Is it the truth according to God's Word? Is it honest or is it contrary to what you know to be truth about God, your life and others? Is it pure or is it tainted by the way the world around you views life? What about things that are lovely, beautiful to behold, of good reputation? Think on things that are virtuous and praiseworthy for these are the things that build us up and determine the lenses through which we view our lives and the lives of others (Philippians 4:8) Anything else is meaningless, *"a chasing after the wind"* (Ecclesiastes 1:14, NIV).

So, make it a regular habit to pause and reflect on what you allow into your mind and if it is healthy for you. The good news is that, just like with your physical diet, if you mess up your spiritual diet, you can always begin again.

Pause for reflection: Do you apply the same care to what you allow into your hearts as you do with your body? Why do you think we care more about our physical appearance than we do about our hearts? Is it because that is what people first see when they meet us?

DAY TWENTY-SEVEN

Sacrificing the promise

*"My covenant will I not break, nor alter the
thing that is gone out of my lips."*
(Psalm 89:34, KJV)

∞

When God appeared to Abraham in a vision, He made a covenant promise to him saying, *"Look up into the sky and count the stars if you can. That's how many descendants you will have"* (Genesis 15:5, NLT)! This was an unbelievable promise to a man and his wife who were well past their child-bearing years. We are told that Abraham believed what God told him and God counted him as righteous because of his great faith (Genesis 15:6). In order to further solidify His promise, God used additional imagery to establish His covenant with Abraham, comparing the multiplication of Abraham's descendants to the sands on the shore (Genesis 22:17).

I try to imagine Abraham looking up every day and waiting for the manifestation of the promise. He was a hundred years old and Sarah ninety before the son of promise arrived. God had begun to fulfill His promise to Abraham that through his seed all the nations of the earth would be blessed. Or so it seemed until God made a demand on Abraham's faith.

God said to Abraham, *"take your son, your only son—yes, Isaac, whom you love so much ... and sacrifice him as a burnt offering on one of the mountains ..."* (Genesis 22:2, NLT). What? How could it be that God was asking Abraham to surrender the same son through whom God's covenant would come to pass? It did not make sense. We know now how the story transpired, but at the time, Abraham did not know what was going to be the outcome of his obedience when he left home that morning with his son and the wood for the sacrifice.

Abraham's surrender of his son is recounted in the Hebrews 11 faith hall of fame. In Hebrews 11:17, we learn more about what transpired that morning. Abraham wrestled in his heart about what God's plan was for his son and arrived at the conclusion that if he offered Isaac as a sacrifice to God, that God was able to bring him back to life. We learn that *"in a sense Abraham did receive Isaac back from the dead"* (Hebrews 11:19, NLT). How? Because when he left home that morning, he had already relinquished his son in his heart and had offered him up for sacrifice by the very act of undertaking the journey in the first place.

God rewarded Abraham's obedience by providing a sacrifice just in the nick of time. And Abraham named the place of this encounter **Jehovah Jireh,** meaning the Lord will provide. Abraham was very sure that his God was a covenant-keeping God, but he did not know how God would reveal this. His obedience to the call that morning opened up the opportunity for God to prove Himself as **El-Shaddai**, the All-Sufficient God.

What is God requiring you to give up today? Is there anything or anyone you hold more dearly in your heart than you do God? Remember this: He is your sufficiency, too, and He is able to provide for your every need. All you have to do is trust Him. Release that thing in your hand or your heart so you can experience Him as Jehovah Jireh.

Pause for reflection: You have read that God is a covenant-keeping God (Numbers 23:19, NLT). Do you really believe this? If not, what is stopping you from completely yielding to this truth?

DAY TWENTY-EIGHT

The waves and winds obey His voice

*"He assigned the sea its boundaries and
locked the oceans in vast reservoirs."*
(Psalm 33:7, NLT)

∞

The world is seeking perfection in many ways, but when we measure perfection by the world's standards, we will always come up short. Why? Because we live in a fallen world where the ground beneath our feet can shift at any moment and for reasons beyond our control. Our lives are not perfect in the popular understanding of that word. Our lives are in the process of being perfected because we serve a perfect God who takes all our imperfections and displays His grace, power and might through them. He does this by keeping us safe in the storm so that we do not drown or become overwhelmed. The Word's standard for perfection does not come from a storm-free life because there is nothing like that. Perfection is when the storms that should drown you wash over you and you are still standing because God shields you in the palm of His hands.

Imagine this for a moment. As the waves rise and hit the shore around you, you are not swept under because He made the waves and commands them and they obey. They can only come so far. And with His mighty hands He scoops you up until the storm and the waves pass. Then He sets you down on solid ground. And though your knees may be wobbly for a while from having tried to fight the currents yourself, you soon find solid footing because He is your strength in the storm.

So the next time you find yourself taking inventory of your life and counting the casualties along the way, remember that your life is still perfect in its imperfections because the one who made you and who keeps you is perfect. Your life, children, marriage, relationships and career are perfect because even though they may go through difficult patches every now and then, God has determined the boundaries of the challenges. So perfection comes in the form of victory in the battle, triumph in the war and the staying power of those who are kept by God.

When Shadrach, Meschach and Abednego came out of the furnace in which they had been thrown by Nebuchadnezzar, we learn that the fire had not touched them. Their hair was not singed nor their clothes scorched. They did not even have the smell of the smoke upon them—all because of the fourth man (God) in the fire with them. This same God has promised:

> *When you go through the deep waters, I will be with you. And when you go through the rivers of difficulty, you will not drown. When you walk through the fire of oppression, you will not be burned up; the flames will not consume you. For I am the Lord, your God, the Holy One of Israel, your Savior* (Isaiah 43: 2-3, NLT)

Therefore, do not be afraid! Do not be dismayed! No matter how things might look in the moment, He still speaks to the storm. Just take Him at His word! Now, that is the perfect place to be!

Pause for reflection: By what standards do you measure your life's successes? Do you ever feel that you can never measure up to the illusive perfection that the world has set as a standard? Have you considered that a true measurement of success is your experience of God's commitment to His promises that He will never leave you alone as you navigate life?

DAY TWENTY-NINE

A sure and steadfast anchor of the soul

"This hope is a strong and trustworthy anchor for our souls. It leads us through the curtain into God's inner sanctuary."
(Hebrews 6:19, NLT)

∞

I don't know about you, but I sometimes find myself still majoring in the minors— *"Will God?"* and *"Can God?"* Sometimes it is *"When God?"* and *"How much longer, God?"* In today's verse, Paul is addressing believers, not unbelievers. He is speaking to people who need reminding to grow up in Christ. When different life circumstances result in doubt and impatience toward God's timing and faithfulness, we need to remember that God can be held to two unchangeable things by which it is impossible for Him to lie (Hebrews 6:18)—His promise and His oath.

When God makes an oath toward us, there is no one greater than Him to swear by, so He swears by Himself. Then we who are recipients of His promise have confidence that His Word is forever settled in heaven and that He will never renege on His promises (Psalm 119:89). So in those moments when we can't seem to find Him or see His hand at work in the affairs of our lives, we must remember this: that there is security in His Word and His oath.

Therefore, we who have fled to him for refuge can have great confidence as we hold to the hope that lies before us" (Hebrews 6:18b, NLT).

This is a hope that is built on the foundation of God's truth which is that He does not lie and if He has said it, He will do it. The answers we need may not come in the manner and timing we desire, but *"this hope is a strong and trustworthy anchor for our souls"* (Hebrews 6:19, NLT).

Of what use is an anchor? During strong winds and rough currents, a ship is securely held down to the ocean floor by an anchor. The ship's crew trusts that the anchor will keep the vessel from drifting away in turbulent weather. The writer of Hebrews describes the hope which lies before us as *"a strong and trustworthy anchor for our souls"* and because of this hope, we can boldly enter through the veil into the Holiest of Holies. When we build our hope on shifting sand, our anchor will not stand. Our hope must be in the unchangeable Word of God which has promised us access in Him to all we need for life.

Pause for reflection: What do you hold on to when you feel there is no hope for you? Do you struggle to trust God and His Word? Hold on to the promises in His Word for they will surely come to pass!

DAY THIRTY

The closer you listen, the more you understand

"Martha, Martha, you are worried and upset about many things."
(Luke 10:41, NIV)

∞

There was a time when I would not have described myself as an anxious person, but recently this fact was brought to the fore. Somewhere beneath my outward calm, there are seeds of anxiety that sprout every now and then. I am also a very analytical person and that personality, coupled with anxiety, make strange companions. The Lord helped me face this reality the morning He whispered to me, *"Chinwe, Chinwe, you are anxious about many things."* He is the God who created me and who can perceive my innermost thoughts. He sees my struggles to make sense of different matters instead of finding my rest in Him alone. Hadn't He admonished another woman this same way? Mary was the sister who sat at His feet, listening to His teachings while the other sister, Martha, rushed around, anxiously trying to understand her sister's choices. *"Martha, Martha,"* Jesus gently called out to her, reminding her to slow down and enjoy the moment.

Martha's frustration was understandable. She was playing a role expected of women in her culture, and she felt comfortable enough with Jesus to complain aloud to Him, even to the hearing of the disciples. Martha thought it was "unfair" of her sister to shirk her share of hosting responsibilities, but Jesus did not encourage her pity party. Instead, He let her know that she, too, could join Mary at His feet. Mary had chosen the better thing which was to sit still and pay close attention to what she was hearing, especially since Jesus had taught that those who listen to His teaching will be given more understanding (Mark 4:24-25).

We are not told whether Martha stopped to join in the fellowship, but today the Lord is calling us to pay close attention to how and what we hear. The closer we listen, the more understanding we will get, and the more we understand, the less anxious we will be. But we cannot listen closely if we are anxious because anxiety is distracting. It is a peace stealer. If we determine to sit still in His presence and pay close attention, then we will find peace. When we come to Him in prayer and surrender our cares to Him, then we are living according to Paul's teaching:

> *Don't worry about anything; instead, pray about everything. Tell God what you need, and thank him for all he has done. Then you will experience God's peace, which exceeds anything we can understand. His peace will guard your hearts and minds as you live in Christ Jesus* (Philippians 4:6-7, NLT)

When anxious thoughts come, turn to your Father and surrender your fears to Him. Then you will be able to calm and quiet yourself like a child weaned from its mother's milk (Psalm 131:2). At the master's feet is where you will find everlasting peace from the Prince of Peace Himself.

Pause for reflection: What types of matters trouble your soul? Have you found that no amount of anxiety or worry can still your troubled soul? Jesus is the Prince of Peace and at His feet you can listen closely, get understanding and find calm for your anxious thoughts.

DAY THIRTY-ONE

Fear of the dark unknown

"She is clothed with strength and dignity,
and she laughs without fear of the future."
(Proverbs 31:25, NIV)

∞

People go to great lengths to catch a glimpse into their future. It seems easier to trust God that way. Psychic readers make a living from reading palms and tarot cards and gazing into crystal balls. Even believers who know better than to consult with psychics still want to know how the future will pan out. The compelling reason is fear of the unknown.

Sometimes, the time span between a promise from God and its fulfillment can seem like eons and create a fear of the unknown. And if you are like me, you keep searching for the fulfillment of God's promise in different events that happen in your life, saying of each event, *"Surely this is what God meant when He said..."* The unknown is scary and our finite minds do not do well with the things we cannot see. Neither do we do well with waiting, but we can count on God to be faithful. Recently God reminded me of His promise:

> *Do not be afraid or discouraged, for the Lord will PERSONALLY go ahead of you [emphasis mine]. He will be with you; he will neither fail you nor abandon you* (Deuteronomy 31:8, NLT)

If God has stepped ahead of us into the future, then that should bring the reassurance we need. God knows the limits of our human understanding of His ways and the fact that we may fear His plans for us, but He wants us to face our fears knowing that He will be by our side. If He has gone ahead, then He is already there when we get there. If He is already there, then there is nothing for us to fear.

In Proverbs 31, we are introduced to a woman who was fearless. Reading about her can be intimidating, but I noticed that she not only wore strength and dignity like a cloak, but that she could laugh boldly at things to come. This means that she was not afraid of the stock market of her time or her real estate investments. She was not overwhelmed with everything she had to do to keep her house in order.

When God, Himself, promises to be with you at all times, then there is nothing left to fear. All you have to do is take Him at His Word that He has already entered your tomorrow ahead of you. You, also, can laugh at the future because of this truth. You do not have to understand everything or see the whole picture before you, too, cloak yourself with strength and dignity like the Proverbs 31 woman.

Pause for reflection: Why do you think it is hard to walk with God and trust that He will take care of your present and future needs? Can you imagine being able to laugh at a future which you cannot yet see? Picture a future with a God who has already gone ahead of you, and then you, too, can laugh.

FINAL REFLECTION

"Let us hear the conclusion of the whole
matter: fear God and keep his commandments:
for this is the whole duty of man."
(Ecclesiastes 12:13, KJV)

∞

One particular year, I could see God's hand leading me through the slow process of practicing forgiveness. Although I could not get my mind to turn off the movie of the offences that were replaying themselves in technicolor and 3-D, I had to make a radical decision to understand and practice how to extend love and grace towards others. My decision was borne out of a desire to please God by loving and serving Him through my loving acts towards others. I also knew that my healing was connected to my repeated obedience to God's commandment: *"And be kind to one another, tenderhearted, forgiving one another, even as God in Christ forgave you"* (Ephesians 4:32, NKJV).

One day, on what looked like any other ordinary spring evening, God graciously allowed me to recall specific sins of mine which He had not only forgiven, but which He had removed *"as far as the east is from the west"* (Psalm 103:12, NKJV). The scenes playing in my mind were from long-forgotten trespasses, now distant in my memory. He caused me to realize that but for His saving grace I was as flawed, if not even more, than the people who have offended me at various times.

Today, I am assured that God has forgiven me because I don't struggle with guilt about my past sins. I deserved to pay the penalty for my sins because He is a Holy and Just God who requires holiness from us; yet, I enjoy the gift of walking in freedom as a justified daughter of the most high God.

I believe God allowed me to remember how much I had been forgiven just to remind me that freely I have received and freely I should give (Matthew 10:8). Here I was, walking all these years in the liberty that faith in Jesus Christ's atonement for my sins had afforded me; yet, I was struggling to accept the humanity of others, failing to recognize that if not for the grace of God, I, too, had the same capacity to hurt others.

I quickly cried out to God and thanked Him for forgiving my sins, past and present. I repented for holding others hostage for what I perceived to be deliberate wrongs against me. I had operated for too long from the stance of "they should have known better" and felt that they did not fully grasp the magnitude of their actions towards me. But in the parable of the king and the servant in Matthew 18, I realize that we will forgive others to the measure of our understanding of how much we have been forgiven. Thankfully, the Word of God shined a light into my situation and reminded me that love does not keep a record of wrongs (1 Cor. 13: 5). This is as true of God's love towards me as it is of my love towards others. If God tallied and kept a record of my transgressions, would I be able to stand?

Are you struggling to forgive anyone today? Do you feel that their actions towards you are unforgiveable? Can you accept God's forgiveness of your sins and remember that *"with the same measure you use, it will be measured back to you"* (Matt. 7:2, NKJV)? Maybe your struggle with forgiveness is because you do not fully comprehend *"what is the width and length and depth and height ... [of] the love of Christ which passes knowledge"* (Ephesians 3:18-19, NKJV). Today you can ask for help from *"Him who is able to do exceedingly abundantly above all that we ask or think, according to the power that works in us"* (Ephesians 3:20, NKJV).

But first, if you have not made Jesus Christ the Lord of your life and accepted the fact that He has paid the penalty for your sins once and for all, you can invite Him into your heart today. It is as simple as praying:

> *Lord Jesus, I am sorry for living a life of rebellion against you. Please forgive my sins. Come into my heart today and make my heart your home. On my own, there is nothing good enough to bring to a Holy God, but I thank you for paying the penalty for my sins so that I am able to stand before God, blameless and without shame. I accept your forgiveness of my sins and, moving forward, I will no longer be held back by fear and condemnation.*

If you are struggling to forgive others, you can begin this journey by praying:

> *My God, I thank you for the revelation that on my own I am powerless to do the right thing, but I can do all things through Christ. Thank you for giving me the gift of your son Jesus Christ. Please help me forgive anyone against whom I hold any grudge. I trust you daily to empower me to walk as your child and to keep your commandment to love you with all my heart and with all my soul and with all my mind* (Matt. 22:37).

Brothers and sisters, now may the joy of the Lord be your strength (Nehemiah 8:10) and may you, with joy, draw waters from the wells of salvation (Isaiah 12:3). Beloved, Christ has come to bring you freedom. Come boldly before

His throne; press in and be ready for the glorious encounter!

In His love,
Chinwe Okpalaoka

www.ingramcontent.com/pod-product-compliance
Lightning Source LLC
Chambersburg PA
CBHW061153040426
42445CB00013B/1667